Out of the Question

Guiding students to a deeper understanding of what they see, read, hear, and do

The process of deciding what is relevant, what is of interest, what is legitimate, what is authentic, and what requires further investigation demands the ability to ask questions.

This book provides both teachers and students with the basics they need to succeed in critically questioning what they see, read, hear, and do.

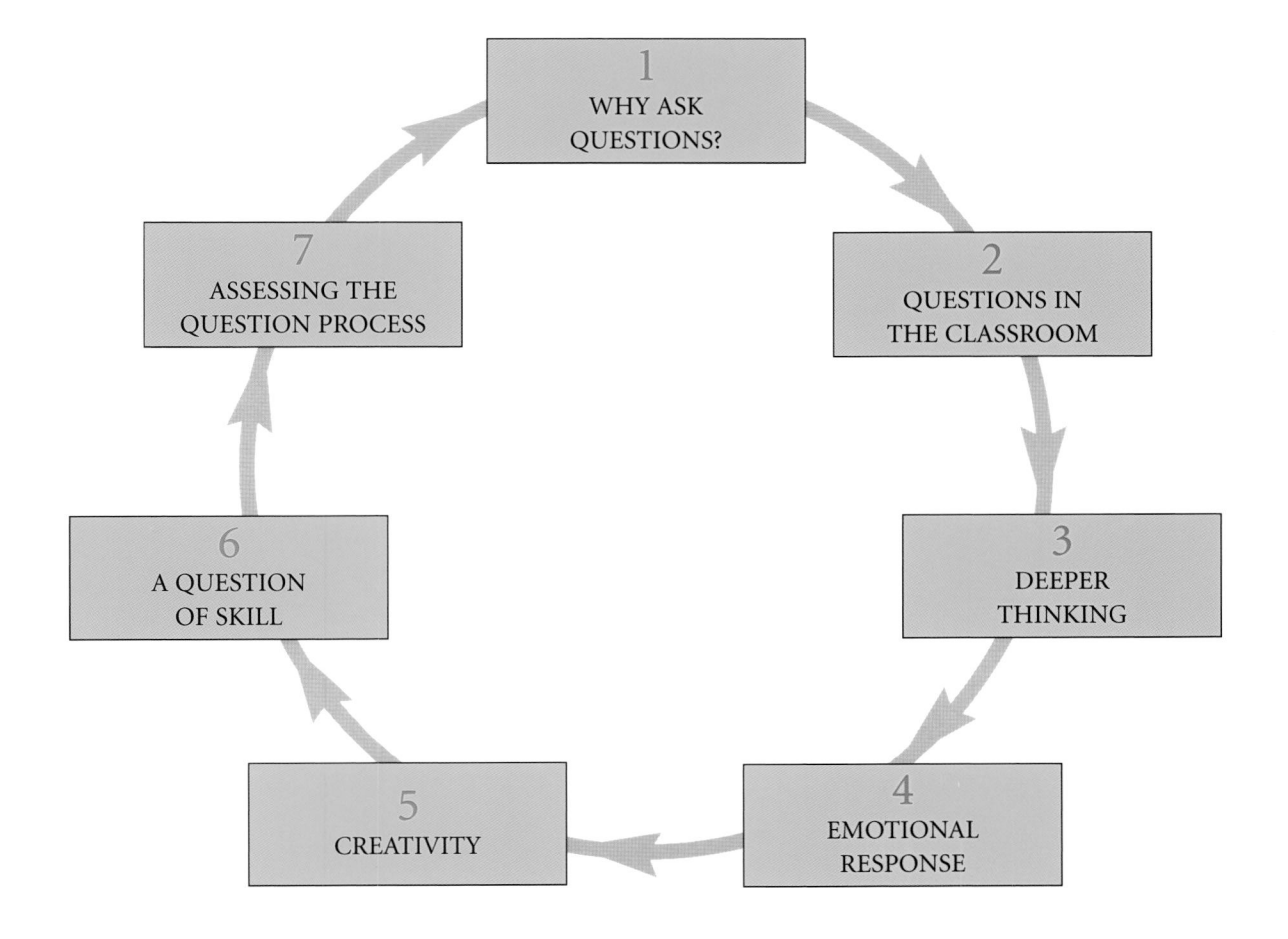

Contents

1. Why Ask Questions?

What Comes "Out of the Question"?   *4*
Effective Questioning   *5*

2. Questions in the Classroom

Questions in Context   *6*
Encouraging Questions and Responses   *7*
Getting Started   *8*
Types of Questions   *9*

3. Deeper Thinking

Self-Questions and Metacognition   *10*
Different Levels of Cognition   *11*

4. Emotional Response

The Affective Domain   *14*
Risk Taking   *15*

5. Creativity

Creative Thinking   *18*
Encouraging Divergent Thinking

6. A Question of Skill

Developing Questioning Skills   *22*

7. Assessing the Questioning Process

Questions about Questioning   *24*
Assessment and Record-keeping   *25*

SUPPORTING STUDENT QUESTIONS   *26*

REPRODUCIBLE PAGES
– Self-Assessment Rubric   *27*
– Assessment Checklist   *28*

RESOURCES   *29*

INDEX   *30*

What Comes "Out of the Question"?

Asking questions is pivotal to learning how to learn and becoming a lifelong learner. In a technology-driven world, where information overload is often an issue, it is essential that people have the skills to critically question what they see, read, and hear. Effective questions support informed decision-making.

Questions help people make sense of the world, and questioning skills empower people as learners. They are pivotal for solving problems, creating solutions, and enacting change. Importantly, asking questions assists students in participating actively in their world and in the wider context of a democratic society.

Questions can

- Excite interest or curiosity
- Direct thinking in a particular way
- Focus attention on a topic
- Encourage active engagement in learning
- Challenge
- Reinforce learned material
- Structure or guide the learning of a task
- Assess
- Encourage reflection on learning
- Help clarify understanding
- Model thinking
- Access a particular type of thinking (e.g., critical, creative, reflective)
- Help make connections
- Spark further questions
- Motivate inquiries
- Identify gaps in learning
- Provide opportunities for learning through discussion

Effective Questioning

Questions should always be driven by purpose and context. When a question engages students and motivates them to ask further questions or challenge their ideas, it has the potential to take students beyond their current thinking.

- Use questions that are predominantly open-ended, thought-provoking, and non-judgmental.
- Plan some questions in advance. Build up to the more challenging questions so that students have time to gain confidence.
- Focus on a few carefully constructed open-ended questions, rather than a quick succession of closed questions.
- Frame questions as clearly and concisely as possible.
- Ask one question at a time.
- Consider the need for think-time. Avoid the trap of answering your own question if students are seemingly slow to respond.
- Vary the strategies used so that questioning does not become predictable.

- Ensure every student has the opportunity to respond to some questions.

Teachers can encourage effective student questions by what they say, and by the ways they provide feedback to student responses, use silence, accept and clarify student questions. Points to consider for helping students to ask effective questions include

- building a shared language for questioning
- introducing different questioning strategies and discussing these with students
- developing student awareness of different types of questions and what type of thinking they require
- making space for student questions and celebrating them.

This book encourages teachers to think about how questioning is critical both for their own learning and their students' learning.

1. WHY ASK QUESTIONS?

Questions in Context

Who asks the questions in a classroom? In some classrooms there is an expectation that the teacher will be the question-asker and students the question-answerers. The classroom culture needs to encourage students to be both question-askers and question-answerers.

Approaches to questioning may vary slightly in accordance with the context—whole class, small group, or individual student.

Whole class Ensuring all students stay engaged can be challenging. In order to manage the whole-class dynamic, control of the questioning process is essential:

• Be inclusive.
• Redirect questions so that several students can respond.
• Summarize responses to keep the class focused.
• Make explicit your expectations about appropriate ways to respond.

Small group Small-group learning offers greater opportunities for students to build their question-asking and question-answering skills. In this context, the teacher can distribute questions more evenly and take the time to assist students in clarifying ideas through exploratory talk. It is also easier for the teacher to step back from a more controlling role and to encourage students to respond to one another.

Students need opportunities to lead their own small-group learning in discussions and group conferences. When students question each other about their learning, it has the potential to generate higher-level thinking.

Individual student One-on-one scenarios in a conference situation provide excellent opportunities for students to reflect on their learning, and for teachers to monitor student learning. Questions need to be carefully framed so that the student doesn't feel a sense of interrogation. In this context, question-asking and question-answering should be viewed as joint responsibilities shared between teacher and student.

Encouraging Questions and Responses

It is important to make explicit your expectations about students being active question-askers. One approach is to jointly construct a chart identifying behaviors associated with a classroom culture that values questions. In response to the prompts *A question-friendly classroom is/is not …*, students write statements about their beliefs and values.

A question-friendly classroom is a place where	A question-friendly classroom is not a place where
• different responses to a question are encouraged • students build on each other's responses • students are prepared to challenge or contest a response • students generate questions for discussions	• student responses to questions are put down • teachers are seen as the question-askers and students as the question-answerers • students recite a response to a question rather than discuss it

The way teachers encourage and receive student responses to questions transmits very explicit messages about their expectations of student learning and the classroom culture. If the purpose of questioning is discussion, directing students to predetermined answers defeats the opportunity of open-ended questions. When students think that a particular answer is required (or valued) it might discourage them from responding to questions honestly. In the following example, the teacher's responses reduce an open-ended question to a closed question with a predetermined answer.

Teacher *What does war cost?*
Student *It costs love.*
Teacher *Yes, good.*
Student *It costs lives.*
Teacher *Costs lives, certainly.*
Student *It costs freedom.*
Teacher *Yes, we had it here. Great point, but you haven't got it.*
Student *Identity.*
Teacher *Good, but it wasn't what I was thinking of. I'll give you a clue. What didn't he have?*
Student *Love.*
Teacher *Partly.*
Student *Childhood and love.*
Teacher *Childhood. That's the one I like.*

Handling Student Responses

Strategy	Description	Application
Demonstrate active listening	Show students you are interested in their response.	Use nonverbal signals, such as facial expressions, a nod, eye contact, sitting forward.
Sustain the question	Use follow-up probes that encourage the clarification, extension, or elaboration of a response. Encourage a range of responses to the one question.	*Could you tell us a little more about that idea? Can you provide some evidence to support your point of view? Does anyone have a different opinion?*
Allow wait-time	Learn to be comfortable with the silences, so that wait-time is extended. Tell students why you are waiting.	Use affirmative nonverbal signals (such as a nod) that show engagement and provide encouragement.
Minimize feedback	Affirm student responses, but avoid excessive praise, which may silence alternative responses.	*That an interesting view. Yes, that's one way. Can anyone add to that? Thank you for that idea.*

Getting Started

The activities and strategies in this book have many possible adaptations and can be used with different age groups.

Topic Dice

Purpose: Evaluate student learning

Write questions related to the current topic on a large cube. One person at a time rolls the die and responds to the question.

Talk and Question Tokens

Purpose: Use of questions to initiate discussion

In a small group, distribute five yellow tokens (responses) and five blue tokens (questions) to each student. Each time a participant responds to a question or makes a comment, a yellow token must be returned to a tub; likewise a blue token when a question is asked. All participants must have the opportunity to use all their tokens.

Types of Questions

A very broad way of categorizing questions is to type them as open or closed. If a question is closed, the answer is non-negotiable and is simply recited; an open-ended question invites interpretation, there being no preconceived response. Open and closed questions are sometimes respectively referred to as divergent and convergent questions, lower-order cognitive and higher-order cognitive questions, or sometimes (in student language) as fat and skinny questions. While there are subtle differences, these terms are often used interchangeably.

Three broad categories that might assist when planning a sequence of questions for a lesson or unit of work are cognitive, affective, and creative. It is essential to make these explicit to students so that they can expand their ways of considering and generating questions, and develop language skills associated with questioning.

Open and Closed Questions
Purpose: Differentiate between open-ended and closed questions

1. Write one topic word on a sticky note for each class member and stick on the student's back. To figure out what is written on their label, students may ask only questions that have a yes or no response. Explain that these questions are "closed" questions, as they don't require students to engage in deeper-level thinking.

Discuss the benefits and disadvantages of questioning in this way. Discuss any strategies the students might have developed to find the answer.

2. Use postcards to demonstrate the way an open-ended question is constructed. As a class, construct five open questions relating to the picture on a postcard. In small groups, students practice writing open questions for their own postcards. Questions and cards are exchanged, and each group uses their postcard and set of questions for a small-group discussion.

2. QUESTIONS IN THE CLASSROOM

Self-Questions and Metacognition

Questions that elicit reflection and metacognition are very important. Some argue that reflection and metacognition are central to learning. They assist in monitoring and self-regulating learning, particularly in student-centred classrooms.

Reflective questions engage the learner/thinker in purposeful consideration of the effectiveness of actions and experiences.

Metacognitive questions focus on the learner's awareness, evaluation, and regulation of their own thinking. When students use metacognition, questions relate to making decisions, choosing appropriate strategies and thinking processes, self-assessing their own thinking, planning action, and setting goals.

Create question strips by copying and cutting apart student questions from the table to the right. Strips can be used to engage students in reflection and metacognition.

Reflective	Examples of Questions
Teacher reflection of teaching practice	What were the strengths of this lesson/unit? What were its weaknesses? How useful were the assessment tasks?
Questions to elicit student reflections	What team skills did your group use? What did you like about the activity?
Student reflection	What did I contribute to the group? What aspects of my work need to be improved? What skills have I improved in this unit?

Metacognitive	Examples of Questions
Teacher metacognition of teaching practice	How can I support students' learning? What did I learn about the way students process information?
Questions to elicit student metacognition	Why might we be studying this topic? What are your big questions? What goals will you set for your learning?
Student metacognition	What do I want to find out? What questions do I have? How will I source the information? What did I learn? What learning strategy worked best for me?

Different Levels of Cognition

Bloom's Taxonomy of cognitive processes is readily adaptable for designing questions that target specific levels of thinking.

Bloom's Taxonomy

Cognitive Level	Processes	Verb Stems
Knowledge ↓ Remembering	Recalling factual information	name, state, define, repeat, list, recall
Comprehension ↓ Understanding	Understanding information	explain, identify, describe, compare, report, outline, tell, locate, review
Application ↓ Applying	Using previous knowledge, concepts, principles, or theories in new situations	apply, practice, use, demonstrate, illustrate, dramatize, interpret
Analysis ↓ Analyzing	Breaking information into parts and showing an understanding between the parts	analyze, contrast, compare, question, debate, relate, examine, identify

Cognitive Level	Processes	Verb Stems
Synthesis ↓ Creating (Switched with Evaluating as the highest level of thinking)	Generating new ideas, planning, and producing	compose, propose, suggest, plan, design, construct, invent, formulate, create, arrange, prepare
Evaluation ↓ Evaluating	Critiquing, making a judgment on the values of consistency of a process, product, or idea	judge, assess, decide, rate, evaluate, measure, estimate, choose

Questions to Encourage Deeper Thinking

Thought-provoking questions provide a useful tool for supporting students to take responsibility for thinking more deeply, and generating more considered responses to questions. These questions require students to clarify, justify, and extend their ideas and opinions.

Fairytales

Purpose: See the different levels of thinking that can be required by a question

Introduce students to the following set of questions designed around Bloom's Taxonomy for the story *Little Red Riding Hood*. Groups of students each take a different fairytale or story and design their own questions.

Remembering	Where did Little Red Riding Hood's grandmother live?
Understanding	What was the purpose of Little Red Riding Hood's visit to her grandmother?
Applying	If your grandmother was sick and you went to visit her, what would you take her?
Analyzing	Why do you think Little Red Riding did not recognize the wolf?
Evaluating	Do you think Little Red Riding Hood's mother behaved responsibly sending her to visit Grandma on her own?
Creating	How might the story have been different if Little Red Riding Hood had her cell phone?

The Q-Matrix

Purpose: The development of questions that target different thinking levels

	Event	Situation	Choice	Person	Reason	Means
Present	What is...?	Where/ when is...?	Which is...?	Who is...?	Why is...?	How is...?
Past	What did...?	Where/ when did...?	Which did...?	Who did...?	Why did...?	How did...?
Possibility	What can...?	Where/ when can...?	Which can...?	Who can...?	Why can...?	How can...?
Probability	What would...?	Where/ when would...?	Which would...?	Who would...?	Why would...?	How would...?
Prediction	What will...?	Where/ when will...?	Which will...?	Who will...?	Why will...?	How will...?
Imagination	What might...?	Where/ when might...?	Which might...?	Who might...?	Why might...?	How might...?

(Adapted from Wiederhold 1995)

Put all the key words onto flashcards. Make two different colored sets: one with *what, where, which, who, why,* and *how;* and another with *is, did, can, would, will,* and *might.* Students select a card from each set and brainstorm all the questions they can think of containing those words.

The Five Whys

Purpose: Use probes to extend a response or acquire more in-depth information

This is a paired activity, in which one person takes the role of questioner and the other answers the questions. After each response, the questioner uses the response to create a new "why" question. Each person needs to listen carefully to the other. The pair aims to ask five questions that get a new, usually more in-depth, answer.

   Five is a random number; it is more important that students listen and think carefully about their questions and responses than that they reach the fifth question. It is interesting to hear where each pair ends up—the final question and response.

Example:
Question: *Why do we have a school cafeteria?*
Answer: *Because people want to buy lunch.*
Question: *Why do people want to buy lunch?*
Answer: *Because they prefer bought lunches to lunches they bring from home.*
Question: *Why do they prefer lunches bought from the cafeteria?*

You Are a Reporter

Purpose: Frame questions that will elicit in-depth information

Students prepare questions to interview a peer. This could be related to things they have been doing at school or home. They can use the questions to survey others and report back on their findings.

Thinking on Your Feet

Purpose: Generate questions to clarify thinking

When students respond to questions in a standing position, more brain cells are activated. Plan some questioning that requires students to be on their feet. For example, create a values continuum ranging from "strongly agree" to "strongly disagree," where students are asked to position themselves in relation to particular statements. Once students are positioned, question them about their stance, encouraging them to be flexible in their thinking and to change positions if convinced by the arguments of their peers.

3. DEEPER THINKING

The Affective Domain

Questions that address our feelings and emotions are associated with the affective domain. They are central to our hearts and souls, and are sometimes referred to as essential questions (McKenzie 2000). These questions probe complex matters that elude simple answers. Examples of these questions include

- What does it mean to have integrity?
- Who do I consider to be somebody with integrity?
- What does it mean to be a good friend?
- Who do I consider to be my good friends?
- How can I be a better friend?

Krathwohl et al's (1964) Affective Domain Taxonomy is concerned with emotional responses, and was designed to complement Bloom's Taxonomy. While not as widely known to educators as Bloom's Taxonomy, its significance should not be overlooked. Chambers (1994), known for his work in developing literature circles and enhancing the quality of student discussion, advocates the importance of starting with questions that address students' emotional responses before moving on to more directed questions. Typical questions would be

- What did you like the most?
- Was there anything you did not like?
- What was something that puzzled you?
- Was there anything that made a pattern?

Instructional Objectives for the Affective Domain

Cognitive Level	Instructional Objectives	Useful Verbs for Framing Questions
Receiving	Listening or attending closely	recall, recognize, observe, select, reply, use, feel, identify, describe
Responding	Showing active interest or enjoyment	answer, assist, compile, discuss, perform, present, tell, label, practise, report
Valuing	Demonstrating commitment, concern, or involvement	complete, form, join, justify, report, share, select, argue, study, persuade
Organization	Constructing a value system	adhere, alter, arrange, combine, compare, define, explain, identify, modify, synthesize, defend, integrate, articulate
Characterization	Acting in accordance with an established value system	discriminate, display, influence, qualify, question, revise, solve, verify, propose, review, judge, resolve, rate, conclude

(Adapted from Krathwohl et al 1964)

Risk Taking

Asking questions and responding can feel risky to students, especially when dealing with issues that carry emotional weight, or when points of view or opinions are in conflict.

It is important for students to learn about responding to each other appropriately, particularly when contesting a peer's response to a question. Reliance on teacher modeling of appropriate ways to challenge an idea or opinion may not always be sufficient. Some explicit teaching of the skills through an activity can help students acquire the language required for framing such responses, and prevent disputational talk.

Providing students with some assistance in rehearsing responses to a contested idea is a useful strategy. For example:

• Have you considered the point of view of...?
• What about considering this point of view...?
• I agree with what you say, but I also think...
• Another way of looking at the situation is...
• Yes, but what would you think if...?
• That's one way, but another possibility is...

Encourage students to develop their own lead-ins to challenging a response. Their examples and the ones listed above could be recorded on a chart or strips and can be used by students during small-group discussions.

Ensuring that students feel comfortable about challenging a response to a question should not be underestimated. Without the necessary skills, students may be reluctant to contribute alternative perspectives and ideas, resulting in conformity or a groupthink approach to discussion. If your aim is for students to explore ideas through open-ended, higher-order questions, they must learn to value a diversity of opinions and ideas.

Wear My Shoes

Purpose: Ask questions that take into account other perspectives and points of view

1. Students try to imagine being in someone else's shoes.

Example:
A war is about to break out in your city. What questions might be asked by local citizens, the military, the families of those in military service, etc.?

2. Alternatively, provide a range of old eyeglasses (lenses removed) and have students wear them as props. Students try to "see" the issue being discussed using different perspectives.

Emotional Questioning

Purpose: Develop questions that encourage emotive responses

Use multiple sets of cards with question types written on them, as follows:

Prediction/ imagination	What if...? What would happen if...? What could happen if...?
Quantity questions	List all the things... How many ways...?
Compare-and-contrast questions	How is it the same? How is it different?
Emotion and motivation	Make 'em laugh; make 'em mad; make 'em sad. (Discuss a controversial issue. Be provocative.)
Point of view	How would an ant feel about an elephant?

Organize the students into small groups. Provide each group with a stimulus picture or an article selected from the newspaper, and a set of question-type cards. Each group prepares at least one question to match each question type. Students can then answer each other's questions.

Considering All Points

Purpose: Challenge or contest a point of view that differs from your own appropriately and respectfully

Create question cards with generic questions.

Examples:
- Why did you say that?
- Is that a good enough reason?
- What are some possible explanations?
- When would that not happen?
- How do you know?
- What would the consequences be?
- Do those two ideas agree?
- How is that different from what was said?
- What questions would be useful to ask?
- What have we learned?

Students prepare posters with controversial statements. Display the posters and discuss why they are likely to produce a range of diverse opinions. Discuss what might have influenced people to develop the views they hold. Students suggest ways they can respond politely to a view with which they disagree. Group members choose a question card to respond to another student's views.

3 Cs and 3 Ps

Purpose: A user-friendly questioning framework that combines the cognitive and affective domains

This questioning model is a practical application of two of Bloom's domains: cognitive and affective. It requires students to critique, compare, make connections, consider a range of perspectives, personalize the issue/idea, and prioritize.

<table>
<tr><th colspan="2">Think about it</th></tr>
<tr>
<td>Critique</td>
<td>What do you know and believe?
What might you expect to happen?
What are all the factors involved?
What are the gaps or silences?
Whose view dominates?
What are the strengths and weaknesses?</td>
</tr>
<tr>
<td>Compare</td>
<td>What if you compare...?
What are the similarities between _____ and _____?
What are the differences between _____ and _____?</td>
</tr>
<tr>
<td>Connect</td>
<td>If you put all the factors together, what are the big ideas?
What are the main ideas?
What relationships can you make?
What are some of the causes and consequences?</td>
</tr>
</table>

<table>
<tr><th colspan="2">Feel it and act on it</th></tr>
<tr>
<td>Ponder perspectives</td>
<td>What is another way of thinking about this?
What perspective is missing?
How would the situation change if...?</td>
</tr>
<tr>
<td>Personalize</td>
<td>If you had to choose _____ what would you decide?
What is your opinion?
What do you care most about?
Who might have a different point of view?
How could you apply your learning to your life?
How does this fit with your thinking when we started the unit?
How does this relate to your situation?
Have you changed your ideas? If so, how and why?
How do your actions influence others?</td>
</tr>
<tr>
<td>Prioritize</td>
<td>What is the most important?
What is the least important?
Which point do you need to address first?
What can you leave until later?</td>
</tr>
</table>

4. EMOTIONAL RESPONSE

Creative Thinking

There are eight processes identified with creative thinking: fluency, flexibility, originality, and elaboration align with the cognitive domain (thinking abilities); curiosity, complexity, risk taking, and imagination with the affective domain (feeling abilities). Higher-order thinking skills and creativity go hand-in-hand.

Processes Associated with Creative Thinking

	Description	Examples
Fluency	Generating many ideas	• Brainstorm different ideas about how technology will change teaching and learning. • List all the ideas you have for reusing damaged CDs.
Flexibility	Generating varied, different, or alternative ideas	• What other perspectives are there to consider? • What other ways could this problem be solved?
Originality	Generating unusual, unique, or new ideas	• A wildcard scenario might be... • What words might you have spoken had you been the first person to step on the moon?

	Description	Examples
Elaboration	Generating enriched, embellished, or expanded ideas	• How could you extend this idea to _____? • If you wanted to get younger children interested in this book, what would you say?
Risk taking	Experimenting with and exploring ideas	• If you took an opposite tack, what might the outcomes be? • If you were forced to flee the country, what experiences might you have?
Complexity	Improving and explaining ideas	• What would happen if we added...? • How could we change the end result?
Curiosity	Pondering and questioning ideas	• What if...? • What if you had wings? • How might the government work differently if children were allowed to vote?
Imagination	Visualizing and fantasizing ideas	• Imagine that... • Imagine that you were the leader of the country for one day. What would you do?

(Adapted from Dalton 1985 & Gross et al 2001)

Encouraging Divergent Thinking

This model includes seven question types that connect across the affective and cognitive domains.

Divergent Thinking Model

Type of Question	Description	Examples
Quantity	Quantitative examination	• How many...? • What examples can you give?
Change	Creative thinking	• What if you...? • What if one element was changed?
Prediction	Hypotheses, possible outcomes	• What might happen if...? • What would your hypothesis be?
Point of view	Give opinion and justify	• What's your opinion? • Could you extend your idea by considering another perspective?
Personal involvement	Personal point of view	• If you were... • What's your point of view?
Comparative association	Compare and contrast	• What are the differences and similarities between...?
Valuing	Feelings	• What is important to you?
Imagination	Visualizing and fantasizing ideas	• Imagine that... • If you were the leader of the country, what would you do?

(Adapted from Dalton 1985)

Creative Questioning

Purpose: Develop questions that encourage creative thinking

Use multiple sets of cards with question types written on them, as follows:

Prediction/ imagination	What if...? What would happen if...? What could happen if...?
Quantity questions	List all the things... How many ways...?
Compare-and-contrast questions	How is it the same? How is it different?
Emotion and motivation	Make 'em laugh; make 'em mad; make 'em sad. (Discuss a controversial issue. Be provocative.)
Point of view	How would an ant feel about an elephant?

Organize the students into small groups. Provide each group with a stimulus picture or an article selected from the newspaper, and a set of question type cards. Each group prepares at least one question to match each question type. Students can then answer each other's questions.

Six Thinking Hats

Purpose: Thinking critically, creatively, and reflectively

De Bono's six-hat thinking is a well-known strategy that encourages different types of thinking. It can be used to review student learning.

Hat	General	English Literature Focus	Math Multiplication tables focus
White	What have you learned?	After reading the introduction, what can you say about the characters and setting?	What have you learned in the last week?
Yellow	What are the highlights of your work?	What would you say are some of the positives of living in this era/place/family?	What multiplication tables do you now know well?
Black	What things could you have done better?	What difficulties do you anticipate for the characters in the future?	What multiplication tables do you need to work on?

Hat	General	English Literature Focus	Math Multiplication tables focus
Red	What do you feel about your accomplishments?	How have your feelings changed about the characters? What issues in the book concerned you?	How do you feel about your progress with learning tables?
Green	What could you have done differently?	If you were the author, how would you have started the story differently?	Is there another way you could learn your tables?
Blue	What would you say about your progress? What questions do you now have?	What issues has the author tackled and ignored? What questions would you like to ask the author?	Overall, what do you think about your understanding of multiplication?

SCAMPER

Purpose: Design questions that encourage creative thinking

SCAMPER—**S**ubstitute, **C**ombine, **A**dapt, **M**odify (Magnify or Minimize), **P**ut to use, **E**liminate, and **R**earrange (or Reverse)—is a useful creative-questioning strategy. Like all strategies, it should not be overused. It should be one of several strategies in the questioning toolbox to encourage creative thinking. Select the techniques that best suit your purposes, rather than use all seven at once. This strategy maybe applied to the study of a text or a unit of work:

• Adapting a product
• Thinking about an issue differently
• Solving a problem more creatively
• Considering alternatives to existing structures, storylines, etc.

(Adapted from Erbele 1972)

Example:

The questions in this sample are designed around the book *The Wishing Cupboard* (Hathorn & Stanley 2002)

S	Substitute	What items would you include in the wishing cupboard?
C	Combine	How might the story be different if Tran and Lan had opened the wishing cupboard together?
A	Adapt	How would you adapt the design of the wishing cupboard to suit your purposes?
M	Modify Magnify	Retell the story from the perspective of the mouse that visited the wishing cupboard. What might Lan add to the wishing cupboard if some drawers were added?
P	Put to another use	What would the wishing cupboard be used for in your home?
E	Eliminate	If all the items were removed, what might the family members now want to include?
R	Reverse	What might have happened if Tran's grandmother had flown with her brother to find the special herb?

5. CREATIVITY

Developing Questioning Skills

The expectation that students will initiate questions must be demonstrated by creating space for student questions within lesson planning:

- When students ask questions, respond positively and attentively.
- Create spaces by remembering to ask: What questions were raised for you by doing this activity? What questions does this text raise? What questions do you have about today's class plan?
- Begin a new topic by asking what questions students have. These can be listed, displayed, and referred to as the topic develops.
- Compile a list of questions students have before beginning a topic discussion.
- Model questions that seek to clarify thinking. Be prepared to express uncertainty and openly question an authoritative text.
- Ask students to use sticky notes to write down questions that come to mind as they read. These can then be brought to class to generate discussion.
- Introduce some games and strategies that build students' skills in constructing questions.

Dos and Don'ts

DO

- Give appropriate feedback for the types of questions you want to encourage.
- Plan questions before the lesson.
- Display questions around the room that capture students' imagination and may challenge them to find the answers.
- Jointly construct lists of great questions that have always puzzled students about things, people, places, events, etc.
- Model self-talk and self-questioning.
- Allow time for students to think of an answer.
- Use student responses to ask further questions.
- Reflect on your techniques and strategies. Consider videotaping a class discussion or eliciting feedback from peers or students.

DON'T

- Ask a string of questions simultaneously.
- Neglect to sustain the question with probes.
- Ask a question and answer it too (rhetorical question).
- Target the same students every time or ask only students you think will give the best responses.
- Use questioning as a behavioral management tool.
- Begin with a very challenging question before students are feeling confident.
- Allow inadequate think-time for higher-order questions.
- Overlook the implications of answers.
- Insist on giving verbal feedback to every answer.

What's in the Box?

Purpose: Develop strategic questioning skills by applying the process of elimination

Place an object in a box and wrap it like a present. Tell students they cannot guess what's in it until they are absolutely sure. They must ask yes-or-no questions about the object until they are secure in their guesses. If they guess incorrectly the game is over.

Example:

Question	Y/N
Is it alive?	No
Was it ever alive?	No
Is it round?	Yes
Is it bigger than a hand?	No
Is it soft?	No
Is it solid?	No
Is it white?	Yes
Is it breakable?	Yes
Is it an egg?	Yes

Celebrity Heads

Purpose: Be a strategic questioner by applying the process of elimination

Select three or four students to sit at the front of the class facing the others. Give each a word they have not seen to place on his or her head. To guess their own words they take turns asking yes-or-no questions of the audience. If they get a yes response, they get the chance to ask another question; a no response means they have to wait until their next turn. The game ends when one person guesses the word on his or her head. A clue might be given at the beginning to narrow the guessing field; e.g., they are all mammals.

Take a Stand

Purpose: Develop skills of asking and answering, and of evaluating responses to questions

The class is divided into three groups. One group must take a position on a problem and another group takes the opposite position. The third group develops a list of questions for both positions. After hearing the responses, the third group must make a considered decision about how the problem might be solved.

Questions about Questioning

When do you tell students the answers?

In student-centred classrooms, students have the major responsibility for posing and finding out the answers to their own questions. If teachers answer their questions, students will not have anything to answer themselves. However, there are situations when teachers should answer student questions to avoid student frustration and to allow them to move forward:

• the necessary resources are unavailable or unsuitable
• students have tried to answer their questions for a reasonable amount of time
• an answer is needed for students to complete the task
• students are becoming frustrated or discouraged by dead ends to their answer seeking
• a simple answer will allow students to proceed onto a more complex task

How do you assess questions?

The type of questions that students ask—such as critical, creative, or reflective questions—are generally assessed informally; for example, through observation of student participation in whole-class and small-group discussions, and through questions students pose for project work, inquiry units, and reflective journal entries. A rubric has been developed for this book (see p. 27); however, rubrics work most effectively when they are jointly constructed by the teacher and students to meet the individual needs of the class.

Audio or videotaping a discussion is particularly useful for assessment of teacher and student questioning.

How do I build questions into my plan?

While questions are asked spontaneously in relation to student comments and lesson outcomes, planning of some key questions or discussion statements can improve the quality of questioning. If an inquiry-based unit is being undertaken, some focus questions can be generated at different stages of the inquiry process. Similarly, planning of specific questions can occur for different stages of a lesson. When planning key questions

• Make questions clear and succinct.
• Sequence questions in a logical order.
• Match questions to students' experience and abilities.
• Focus on eliciting higher-order thinking, generalizing, and conceptualizing rather than recalling factual information.

Generic questions for stages of a unit/lesson
Beginning
What do you need to do/know to get the task done?
What different methods/approaches could be useful?
How does this task connect with other tasks you have done?
How will you ensure everybody contributes to the task?

During
What do you remember from last time that may be helpful?
How are you progressing?
Do you need to change your strategies?
What information do you still need?

End
What achievements are you most proud of?
What is something that has taken your interest?
What is something new that you have learned?
What is something that still confuses or puzzles you?

What if students don't ask good questions?

Ask any parent and they will tell you that children ask endless and complex questions. However, they may be reluctant to do so at school. The following ideas might encourage student questioning:

- Model interesting and varied questions.
- Make time for questions throughout the lessons.
- Instead of asking students questions, tell them the answers and have them pose appropriate questions.
- Display questions around the room with the answers that have been found by students.
- Create situations that arouse student curiosity.
- Initiate awards for the best questions. Categories could be determined by the class.
- Use student questions for discussions.
- Ask questions that make students want/need to seek outside of the classroom.
- Discuss different types of questions and identify them when used.
- Have students design quizzes for others.
- Use questioning taxonomies and strategies to structure and vary questions.
- Play games with questions.

Assessment and Record-keeping

Some formal record keeping is useful for assessing the development of students' questioning strategies and skills, and for evaluating the effectiveness of the teaching focus on questioning. While ongoing monitoring may occur informally, evidence is needed to demonstrate student improvement, albeit in a qualitative way, to parents and for school record-keeping purposes.

Sticky notes may be helpful for anecdotal observations about the type of questions students initiate and their responsiveness to questions in small-group and whole-class discussions. Notes can then be transferred to formal record-keeping procedures. A reproducible for record-keeping is provided on page 28, and the rubric on page 27 is an alternative way in which students can self-assess their achievements.

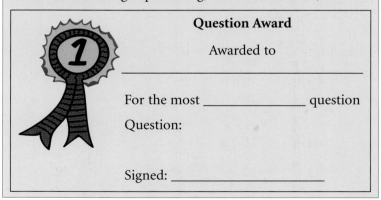

Question Awards
Purpose: Celebrate and encourage effective questioning

Students generate questions that might be nominated as most creative, most thought-provoking, most controversial, etc.

Question Award

Awarded to

_____

For the most _____ question

Question:

Signed: _____

Teachers should think about the types of questions they would ask as part of the planning process. The following checklist may be useful to help reflect on the strategies, structures, and support given to developing effective questions in the classroom.

	Usually	Sometimes	Never
Do I model a variety of questions and questioning strategies?	☐	☐	☐
Do I think about the purpose of the question?	☐	☐	☐
Do I include questions when planning?	☐	☐	☐
Do I make time for students to ask questions and find out the answers for themselves?	☐	☐	☐
Have I organized opportunities for students to adopt different questioning roles?	☐	☐	☐
Do I use students' prior knowledge to help further their ideas?	☐	☐	☐
Do I encourage students to discuss their thinking?	☐	☐	☐
Do I show that I am interested in different types of questions?	☐	☐	☐
Do I use self-assessment to elicit self-questioning?	☐	☐	☐
Do I use probing questions rather than just accepting the first answer to questions?	☐	☐	☐
Do I explain why I asked a particular question?	☐	☐	☐
Do I verbalize questions about my own actions?	☐	☐	☐
Do I encourage students to listen to each other and ask questions of each other?	☐	☐	☐
Do I encourage students to listen to a range of possible answers?	☐	☐	☐
Have I established an environment where students feel free to ask questions and take risks?	☐	☐	☐
Do I allow wait-time for students to answer questions?	☐	☐	☐
Do I listen to student ideas and build on their responses?	☐	☐	☐

SELF-ASSESSMENT RUBRIC

Name: _____

Circle the description that applies to you.

Question-asking	I always ask questions confidently; to clarify my thinking; to seek more information; to critically analyze information; and to get feedback from others.	I usually ask questions confidently; to clarify my thinking; to seek more information; to critically analyze information; and to get feedback from others.	I sometimes ask questions confidently; to clarify my thinking; to seek more information; to critically analyze information; and to get feedback from others.	I never ask questions confidently; to clarify my thinking; to seek more information; to critically analyze information; or to get feedback from others.
Question-answering	I always use think-time when responding to complex questions; respect different ideas; and am flexible in my thinking.	I usually use think-time when responding to complex questions; respect different ideas; and am flexible in my thinking.	I sometimes use think-time when responding to complex questions; respect different ideas; and am flexible in my thinking.	I never use think-time when responding to complex questions; respect different ideas; or am flexible in my thinking.
Question types	I always consider the purpose for my question; and use different types of questions for different purposes.	I usually consider the purpose for my question; and use different types of questions for different purposes.	I sometimes consider the purpose for my question; and use different types of questions for different purposes.	I never consider the purpose for my question; or use different types of questions for different purposes.
Planning	I always use questions to assist in the planning, organizing, and reviewing of my work.	I usually use questions to assist in the planning, organizing, and reviewing of my work.	I sometimes use questions to assist in the planning, organizing, and reviewing of my work.	I never use questions to assist in the planning, organizing, or reviewing of my work.
Self-monitoring	I always ask questions to check my progress; assess my learning; make connections between ideas; and set future goals.	I usually ask questions to check my progress; assess my learning; make connections between ideas; and set future goals.	I sometimes ask questions to check my progress; assess my learning; make connections between ideas; and set future goals.	I never ask questions to check my progress; assess my learning; make connections between ideas; or set future goals.
Risk taking	I am always prepared to ask questions about tentative ideas; to ask creative questions; and to challenge ideas different from mine.	I am usually prepared to ask questions about tentative ideas; to ask creative questions; and to challenge ideas different from mine.	I am sometimes prepared to ask questions about tentative ideas; to ask creative questions; and to challenge ideas different from mine.	I am never prepared to ask questions about tentative ideas; to ask creative questions; or to challenge ideas different from mine.

An effective question I recently asked: _____

Two aspects of questioning I want to improve: _____

• _____

• _____

My plan of action is _____

ASSESSMENT CHECKLIST

Name: _____

	OFTEN	SOMETIMES	NEVER	COMMENTS
Question-asking				
Asks questions confidently				
Initiates questions in a discussion context				
Asks clarification questions				
Asks divergent questions				
Asks questions to extend understanding				
Directs questions to peers				
Asks questions to get feedback from others				
Takes risks with question-asking				
Asks critically analytical questions				
Question-answering				
Takes think-time before answering complex questions				
Is prepared to explore tentative ideas				
Contests ideas and opinions appropriately				
Respects that people have different perspectives and points of view				
Planning				
Uses effective questions to focus an investigation				
Uses questions to organize an approach to a task				
Uses questions to review work				
Self-monitoring				
Uses questions to self-regulate and monitor progress				
Uses questions to make connections between ideas				
Uses reflective questions to assess learning				

RESOURCES

Abbott, C. and S. Godinho (2001) *Thinking Voices: Developing Oral Communication Skills* Carlton, AU: Curriculum Corporation

Armstrong, Tricia (2003) *The Whole-Brain Solution* Markham, ON: Pembroke

Booth, David (2005) *Story Drama*, 2nd ed. Markham, ON: Pembroke

Charlton, Beth Critchley (2005) *Informal Assessment Strategies* Markham, ON: Pembroke

Chambers, A. (1994) *Tell Me: Children, Reading and Talk* NSW, AU: PETA

Cole, A. (2002) *Better Answers* Portland, ME: Stenhouse

Dalton, J. (1995) *Adventures in Thinking* South Melbourne, AU: Nelson

Dantonio, Marylou and Paul C. Beisenherz (2000) *Learning to Question: Questioning to Learn* Columbus, OH: Allyn & Bacon

de Bono, E. (1992) *CoRT Thinking: Teacher's Notes* Elmsford, NY: Pergamon Press

Erbele, R.F. (1972) "Developing education through SCAMPER" *Journal of Creative Behaviour*, vol 6, pp 192–203.

Gardner, H. (1999) *The Disciplined Mind: What All Students Should Understand* New York, NY: Simon & Shuster

Gear, Adrienne (2006) *Reading Power* Markham, ON: Pembroke

Gross, M. et al (2001) *Gifted Students in Primary Schools: Differentiating the Curriculum* Sydney, AU: A Generic Publication, University of NSW

Harvey, Stephanie and Anne Goudvis (2007) *Strategies that Work*, 2nd ed. Portland, ME: Stenhouse

Hathorn, L. and E. Stanley (2002) *The Wishing Cupboard* South Melbourne, AU: Lothian Books

Hoyt, Linda (2004) *Spotlight on Comprehension* Portsmouth, NH: Heinemann

Hubbard, R. and B. Power (1999) *Living the Questions: A Guide for Teacher-Researchers* Portland, ME: Stenhouse

Koechlin, Carol and Sandi Zwaan (2006) *Q Tasks* Markham, ON: Pembroke

Krathwohl, D., B. Bloom and B. Masior (1964) *Taxonomy of Educational Objectives: The Classification of Educational Goals: Handbook 2. Affective Domain* New York, NY: McKay

Lundy, Kathleen Gould (2007) *Leap Into Literacy* Markham, ON: Pembroke

McGregor, Tanny (2007) *Comprehension Connections* Portsmouth, NH: Heinemann

McKenzie, Jamie (2000) *Beyond Technology* Bellingham, WA: FNO Press

McKenzie, Jamie (2005) *Learning to Question to Wonder to Learn* Bellingham, WA: FNO Press

Morgan, Norah and Juliana Saxton (2006) *Asking Better Questions*, 2nd ed. Markham, ON: Pembroke

Swartz, Larry (2002) *The New Dramathemes* Markham, ON: Pembroke

Tovani, Cris (2000) *I Read It But I Don't Get It* Portland, ME: Stenhouse

Wilson, J. and Jan L. Wing (1993) *Thinking for Themselves: Developing Strategies for Reflective Learning* South Yarra, AU: Eleanor Curtain Publishing

Wiederhold, C. with S. Kagan (1995) *Cooperative Learning and Higher-Level Thinking: The Q-Matrix* San Juan Capistrano, CA: Kagan Cooperative Learning

(Activity titles are in italics)

3 Cs and 3 Ps, 17

Affective domain, 14, 17, 18, 19
  Instructional objectives, 14
Affective Domain Taxonomy, 14
Allowing wait-time, 8
Analyzing, 11, 12
Applying, 11, 12
Assessment, 25
  Checklist, 28

Bloom's Taxonomy, 11, 12, 14, 17

Celebrity Heads, 23
Classroom culture, 7
Cognition
  Different levels of, 9, 11, 14
Cognitive domain, 17, 18, 19
Compare, 17
Complexity, 18
Connect, 17
Considering All Points, 16
Context
  Individual student, 6
  Small group, 6
  Whole class, 6
Creating, 11, 12
Creating space, 22
Creative Questioning, 19
Creative thinking, 18, 19
Critique, 17
Curiosity, 18

Demonstrating active listening, 8
Discussion, 8
Divergent thinking model, 19

Elaboration, 18
Emotional Questioning, 16
Evaluating, 11, 12

Fairytales, 12
Feeling abilities, 18
The Five Whys, 13
Flexibility, 18
Fluency, 18

Imagination, 18
In-depth information
  Acquiring, 13
  Eliciting, 13

Metacognition, 10
Minimizing feedback, 8

Open and Closed Questions, 9
Originality, 18

Personalize, 17
Planning, 27, 28
Ponder perspectives, 17
Prioritize, 17
Process of elimination, 23

The Q-Matrix, 12
Question Awards, 25
Question strips, 10, 15
Questioning
  Approaches to, 6
  Developing skills, 22, 23
  Dos and don'ts, 22
  Effective, 5, 25
  Emotional, 16
  Encouraging, 5
  Framework/model, 17
  Planning, 13
  Process, 6
  Purpose, 7
  Questions about, 24
  Skills, 4, 22, 23
  Strategic, 23
  Strategy, 21
Questions
  About questioning, 24
  Accepting, 5
  Affective, 9, 14
  Answering, 6, 23, 27, 28
  Asking, 4, 5, 6, 7, 15, 22, 23, 27, 28
  Categorizing, 9
  Change, 19
  Clarifying, 5
  Closed, 5, 7, 9
  Cognitive, 9
  Comparative association, 19
  Compare-and-contrast, 16, 19
  Compiling, 22
  Constructing, 22
  Context, 6
  Convergent, 9
  Creative, 9, 19
  Deeper thinking, 11
  Designing, 11, 12, 21
  Developing, 15, 19
  Distributing, 6
  Divergent, 9
  Effective, 4, 5
  Emotion and motivation, 16, 19
  Encouraging, 5, 7, 11
  Framing, 5, 6, 13
  Generating, 13
  Generic, 16, 24
  Helping students to ask, 5
  Higher-order cognitive, 9, 15
  Imagination, 16, 19
  Initiating, 22
  Lower-order cognitive, 9
  Metacognitive, 10
  Modelling, 22
  Non-judgmental, 5
  Open-ended, 5, 7, 9, 15
  Personal involvement, 19
  Planning, 5, 22, 27, 28
  Point of view, 16, 19
  Prediction, 16, 19
  Quantity, 19
  Reflective, 10
  Result of, 4
  Rhetorical, 22
  Sequence, 9
  Student, 5, 22
  Supporting student, 26
  Sustaining, 8
  Thought-provoking, 5, 11
  Types, 9, 19, 27
  Valuing, 7, 19

Record keeping, 25
Reflection, 10
Remembering, 11, 12
Responses/responding, 15, 22
  Challenging, 15
  Emotive, 16
  Encouraging, 7
  Evaluating, 23
  Extending, 13
  Handling student, 8
  Rehearsing, 15
Risk taking, 15, 18, 27

SCAMPER, 21
Self-assessment rubric, 27
Self-monitoring, 27, 28
Self-questions, 10
Six Thinking Hats, 20
Student learning
  Evaluating, 8
  Reviewing, 20

Take a Stand, 23
Talk and Question Tokens, 8
Think-time, 5
Thinking
  Clarifying, 13, 22
  Creative, 18, 19, 20, 21
  Critical, 20
  Divergent, 19
  Encouraging, 19
  Reflective, 20
Thinking abilities, 18
Thinking on Your Feet, 13
Topic Dice, 8

Understanding, 11, 12

Wear My Shoes, 15
What's in the Box?, 23

You Are a Reporter, 13

Pembroke Publishers
538 Hood Road
Markham, Ontario, Canada L3R 3K9
www.pembrokepublishers.com

Distributed in the U.S. by Stenhouse Publishers
477 Congress Street
Portland, ME 04101
www.stenhouse.com

This edition is adapted from a book originally titled *How to Succeed with Questioning*, published in 2004 in Australia by Curriculum Corporation — www.curriculum.edu.au

We acknowledge the financial support of the Government of Canada through the Book Publishing Industry Development Program (BPIDP) for our publishing activities.

We acknowledge the Government of Ontario through the Ontario Media Development Corporation's Ontario Book Initiative.

Library and Archives Canada Cataloguing in Publication

Godinho, Sally
Out of the question : guiding students to a deeper understanding of what they see, read, hear, and do / Sally Godinho and Jeni Wilson.

Includes index.
Originally published under title: How to succeed with questioning.
ISBN 978-1-55138-214-2

1. Questioning. 2. Teaching. 3. Learning. I. Wilson, Jeni II. Title.

LB1027.44.G63 2007   371.102   C2007-901520-4

Editors: Kat Mototsune, Rebecca Hill
Cover Design: John Zehethofer
Typesetting: Jay Tee Graphics Ltd.

Printed and bound in Canada
9 8 7 6 5 4 3

Acknowledgements

Many of the examples in this book were inspired by practicing classroom teachers. Others have been developed or published with our dear friends and colleagues. We thank them for their generosity and acknowledge the contributions of Colleen Abbott, Karen Biggeleau, Dee Clements, Robyn English, Kath Murdoch, Susan Wilks, Teresa Stone, and Lesley Wing Jan. Thanks to the teachers of Ballan P.S.

Special thanks to Carol Koechlin for her contribution to this edition.

Out of the Question provides teachers with starting points for establishing a "question-friendly classroom." Each step in this handy book helps students and teachers learn strategically as they explore layers of questioning and practical applications for understanding their respective worlds more fully.

Carol Koechlin, co-author of **Q Tasks**

Asking questions, when you care about the answers, is pivotal to learning how to learn. This 32-page flipchart encourages you to critically question what you see, read, hear, and do. Easy and inviting, **Out of the Question** explores the key issues:

- Why ask questions?
- Nurturing questions in the classroom
- Promoting deeper thinking
- Generating an emotional response
- Encouraging creativity
- Building questioning skills
- Assessing the question process

At the root of this practical book are activities to help you recognize effective questions that help you decide what is relevant, what is of interest, what is legitimate, what is authentic, and what requires further investigation. From the responsibilities of both teacher and student in question-asking and question-answering, to the structure of questions, to a rubric and checklist for assessing the process, this book is a quick and easy reference to the basics.

Pembroke Publishers Limited
538 Hood Road
Markham, ON L3R 3K9 Canada
www.pembrokepublishers.com

Front Cover Photo: Don Farrall /Photodisc Red / Getty Images

ISBN 978-1-55138-214-2

9 781551 382142

Building **Info Smarts**

How to work with all kinds of information and make it your own

RESEARCH NOTES

From reading books and analyzing a movie to working on a research project and solving problems you care about!

This package of learning tools was assembled just for you. *Building Info Smarts* is filled with strategies for learning success at school, at home, at work, at play, and in your community. It can help you discover the foundations of your learning style, construct your literacy skills, impress your teachers with your presentations, explore emerging new technologies, and reflect on your discoveries and successes.

1 WAYS OF LEARNING

2 EXPLORING TO LEARN

3 READING TO RESEARCH

4 FROM INFORMATION TO LEARNING

5 LEARNING TOGETHER

6 LEARNING FOR LIFE

Contents

Ways of Learning
How Do You Learn Best? *4*
Learning Responsibly *5*

Exploring to Learn
Getting Started *6*
   Questions to Explore *7*
   Your School Library *9*

Reading to Research
Actively Read/View/Listen *10*
   Choosing Resources *11*
   Connecting to What You Read/View/Listen *12*
   Reading Smart *14*
   People as Resources *16*
   Using the Resources You Find *16*

From Information to Learning
Building Understanding *18*
Using Graphic Organizers *19*
   Organizing

Comparing
Ordering
Drawing Conclusions
Making a Decision
Finding Solutions
Reviewing for Study

Learning Together
Creating Something New *22*
   Working with Others *23*

Learning for Life
Using Learning Skills Everyday *26*

Using Your Info Smarts
A Workout for Your Brain *28*
   Get Info Smart *28*

Web Resources *29*

Index *30*

How Do You Learn Best?

Everyone learns in a different way. You need to find the way that works best for you.

Outside of School

The activities you enjoy are a very important part of who you are and how you learn. Think about how you spend your time at home, at school, and in your community.

- **First**, brainstorm topics like

Favorite activities	Favorite books	What scares you
Responsibilities	Favorite people	What excites you
Favorite songs	What makes you	Your goals
Favorite movies	happy or sad	Your wishes

- **Take** the information and create a visual representation: a web, collage, photo essay, or combination of visuals.
- **Analyze** your visual profile: What am I best at? Do I do variety of things? What haven't I tried yet? Where do I need to improve?
- **Finally**, target some goals: I think I should try… . I want to…. Perhaps I could learn to…. I will….

Build a Learning Profile

Discover your strengths and target areas to improve your learning potential. Update your profile often.

	Not Much		This is Me!	
I am good at physical activities.	1	2	3	4
I am good at music.	1	2	3	4
I make good observations.	1	2	3	4
I enjoy drawing and painting.	1	2	3	4
I ask a lot of questions.	1	2	3	4
I am good at organizing things.	1	2	3	4
I am good at math.	1	2	3	4
I enjoy science activities.	1	2	3	4
I like working with animals.	1	2	3	4
I enjoy learning about nature.	1	2	3	4
I like working with words.	1	2	3	4
Partner work energizes me.	1	2	3	4
I think about how I am learning.	1	2	3	4
I am good at reading.	1	2	3	4
I like writing stories and reports.	1	2	3	4
I like a challenge.	1	2	3	4

Learning Responsibly

> Learning is a process equation.
> Effort + Strategies = Successful Learning

When you are working with information and ideas, you will always be successful if you boost your effort and work at trying out different strategies.

Keep a Learning Log

- What did I learn today?
- What did I try hard to do today?
- What mistakes did I make?
- What can I learn from those mistakes?
- What strategies did I try?
- Which strategies helped the most?
- How can I improve?
- How can our group improve?
- Why is my new learning important?

Study and Work Smart

The first step in working smart is knowing what is expected. Sometimes you are asked to create a written product:

- an **essay** expresses an idea or an opinion.
- a **story** is a work of fiction.
- a **report** is a presentation of facts.
- a **review** is an evaluation of a book, film, or article.
- a **summary** is a brief overview.
- a **project** requires a learning process over time.

Know Your Teacher's Expectations

- When is my project/assignment due?
- Can I choose my own presentation format?
- Who will my audience be?
- What has to be handed in for assessment?
- What are the assessment criteria?
- How many sources am I expected to use?
- Will I be working with others?
- Am I expected to complete everything at school?

Getting Started

Explore Your Topic

Research is a process. These questions will help you develop a plan for success.

- What is your research focus?
- Why do you want to explore this topic?
- What do you know already and what do you need/want to find out?

To get a big picture of all the components of a broad topic you need to do some pre-research activities and explore data.

- Skim, scan, and read books, magazines, newspapers, and Internet sites.
- Listen to what experts have to say.
- View video clips and photographs, charts, maps, graphs.
- Discuss what you are finding with your classmates.
- Ask lots and lots of questions.

Work with a partner or small group to make a web or mind map of your topic. As you explore you will

- learn new words, phrases
- ask more questions
- make new connections
- cluster ideas

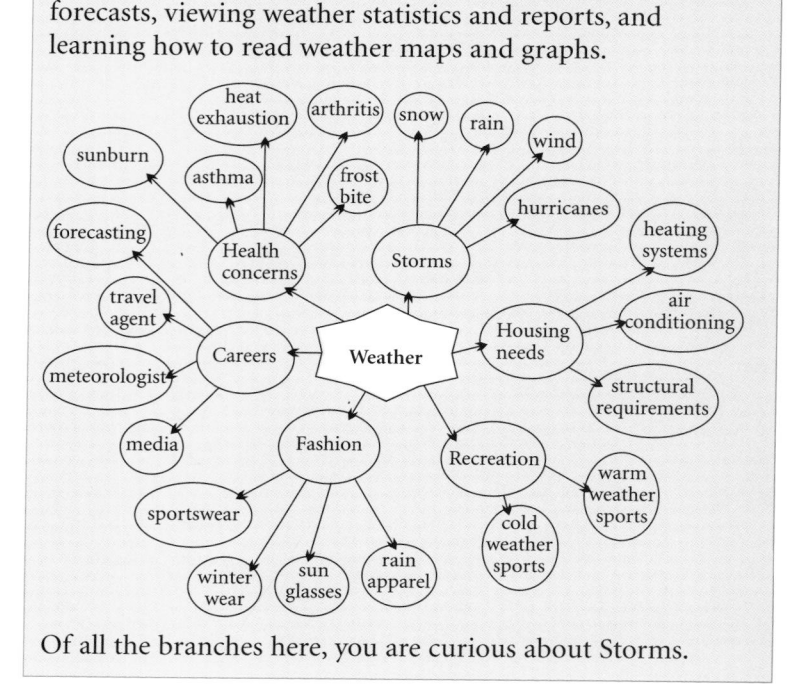

Let's consider the broad topic of **weather**. Exploring weather-related data might involve listening to weather forecasts, viewing weather statistics and reports, and learning how to read weather maps and graphs.

Of all the branches here, you are curious about Storms.

Narrow Your Topic

Examine your web and try to focus on the aspect of the topic that really is of interest to you. Use an organizer to help you get started.

Storms is still a big topic. Let's narrow the topic to hurricanes.		
Topic: Hurricanes		
What do you know?	**What do you need to know?**	**Where can you find out?**
severe winds flooding damage and death Katrina tropical storms evacuation	What are the causes? How is the path predicted How do you prepare/protect yourself? Are they getting worse?	libraries books Internet weather channel weather agencies newspaper databases and archives
Keywords: hurricanes, tropical storms, meteorology, Katrina		

You can apply this process to making all kinds of decisions: from making plans for the weekend to researching summer camps or making a big purchase.

Questions to Explore

For rich rewards, develop a research question that
- stimulates your curiosity
- encourages you to dig deep for information
- challenges you to think about your discoveries
- keeps you on track

Question Prompts

Starting Questions and Statements of Purpose

Who	When	Investigate	Determine
What	Why	Study	Examine
Where	How	Compare	Uncover

Focus on a Topic

Purpose	Types	Result	Relationships
Function	Rates	Importance	Adaptations
Capacity	Structure	Characteristics	Conditions

Look for Relationships

Project	Trends	Contrast	Correlation
Implication	Consequence	Cause	Value
Pattern(s)	Compare	Effect	Analyze

Use Focus or Relationship words to give your question research power.

Research Questions Step-by-Step

- If you are looking for just the facts, build simple questions.
- If you want to uncover understanding, build powerful research questions.
- Statements of purpose are also good research guides.

Weather Questions
Simple Questions
What is a hurricane?

Where do hurricanes occur most often?

Powerful Research Questions
What **causes** hurricanes?

What is the **impact** of hurricanes on people, animal life and the environment?

What are the **consequences** of hurricanes for families and businesses?

How have building/construction methods been **affected** by hurricanes?

Statements of Purpose
Study the role meteorology plays in hurricane areas.

Examine population patterns in areas prone to hurricanes.

Investigate if there is a **correlation** between global warming and tropical storms.

Question Stretchers
Surface Questions

	Who	What	Where	When
is				
did				

Digging Questions

	Who	What	Where	When
can				
would				

Deeper Questions

	Who	What	Where	When
will				
might				

Questions for Developing Understanding

	is	did	can	would	will	might
How						
Why						

Your School Library

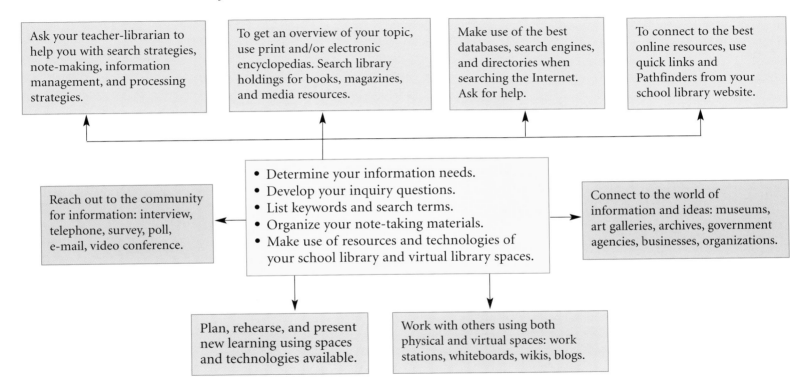

Ask your teacher-librarian to help you with search strategies, note-making, information management, and processing strategies.

To get an overview of your topic, use print and/or electronic encyclopedias. Search library holdings for books, magazines, and media resources.

Make use of the best databases, search engines, and directories when searching the Internet. Ask for help.

To connect to the best online resources, use quick links and Pathfinders from your school library website.

Reach out to the community for information: interview, telephone, survey, poll, e-mail, video conference.

- Determine your information needs.
- Develop your inquiry questions.
- List keywords and search terms.
- Organize your note-taking materials.
- Make use of resources and technologies of your school library and virtual library spaces.

Connect to the world of information and ideas: museums, art galleries, archives, government agencies, businesses, organizations.

Plan, rehearse, and present new learning using spaces and technologies available.

Work with others using both physical and virtual spaces: work stations, whiteboards, wikis, blogs.

EXPLORING TO LEARN

Actively Read/View/Listen

Learning is about understanding. Here are some strategies to help you build understanding of what you read, view, and listen to. Try them on different kinds of texts and media.

Nonfiction
- Skim and scan for an overview.
- Read for subtopics: titles, captions, sidebars, etc.
- Read for needed detail: text, photos, illustrations, etc.

Fiction
- Ask questions.
- Make connections to text, author, and the world.
- Make predictions.

Visuals
- Which details are important?
- What is new information for me?
- Why is this visual important?

Video
- View once for an overview.
- View again and pause to make notes.
- Pay attention to images, words, music; note film techniques.

Listen
- Stop all other activities and focus on the audio.
- Think about the message/facts. Reflect on the emotions.
- Prepare questions

Internet Checklist

Avoid aimless surfing and site-hopping
- ❏ Develop questions to guide your search.
- ❏ Break down your topic into chunks/subtopics.
- ❏ Develop keywords and key phrases.
- ❏ Use search operators to narrow your search.
- ❏ Select the sites you think are best; write down the URLs or bookmark them.
- ❏ Validate your selected websites.

Avoid getting lost in a sea of information
- ❏ Apply your active reading, viewing, and listening skills
- ❏ Investigate visuals like charts and graphs.
- ❏ Don't get sidetracked by animation tricks and glitz.
- ❏ Skim and scan for your keywords and subtopics.
- ❏ When links are off topic, use the Back button to return
- ❏ If you get lost, look for a link to the main/home page and start again.

Avoid the threat of accidental plagiarism
- ❏ Process data as you navigate.
- ❏ Record your findings on an organizer as you go along.
- ❏ Record all direct quotes you plan to use.
- ❏ Record all referencing information.

Choosing Resources

Sometimes deciding what you want or need to read is a problem. Copy these bookmarks and take them with you on your next library visit. The more you read the better reader you will become.

Book Check

Are you just browsing?
- Have you checked out a magazine lately?
- What about a joke book?
- Find books of puzzles and games.
- Do you like reading about famous people?
- Think about other things you are interested in: sports, cooking, movies, crafts, etc.
- Search your library catalogue for a topic of interest.
- Check out the New Book display.
- Ask friends what they have read.
- Ask your teacher-librarian for help.
- Sit down and browse and read.

Found a keeper? **Check it out!**

Book Check

Are you looking for a novel?
- Do you know the author/illustrator?
- Read reviews/synopsis on the back cover.
- Read book jacket flaps.
- Does the genre interest you?
  Mystery
  ✔ Adventure
  ✔ Fantasy
  ✔ Science fiction
  ✔ Historical fiction
  ✔ Contemporary
- Read the first paragraph to check interest.
- Skim a few pages for readability.

Too difficult/easy or not interested?
Try another book.
Looks great? **Check it out!**

Book Check

Looking for quick facts?
- dates
- places
- statistics
- people

Try…
- Atlas
- Encyclopedia
- Almanac
- Yearbooks

Need something for a project?
- Search catalogue using keywords.
- Check table of contents and index for your keywords.
- Skim for headings, subheadings, and captions.
- Check for illustrations, charts, maps, and other visuals related to your research needs.

Too difficult/easy or not interested?
Try another book.
Perfect? **Check it out!**

Connecting to What You Read/View/Listen

Making Connections to Fiction

Think about what makes a good story or movie, then try some of these strategies to help you make connections.

Use a Visual to Map the Story

- Who are the characters? What are they like?
- Where does the story happen? What makes this a good setting?
- How does the story start? What happens next?
- What are the problems? What is the message?

Relate to Characters

- Who would be a good friend, parent, teacher, etc.? Why?
- Who would you like (not like) to be? Why?
- Who do you admire, fear, laugh at, worry about, etc. Why?
- Who needs some advice? What advice?

Think about Solutions

- Solve Problems: What is the problem? How was it caused? Who is it a problem for? How could it be solved?
- Make Predictions: Find hints and clues.
- Solve Mysteries: Clue + evidence + suspect + motive = prediction /solution

Connecting to Feelings

What feelings did you experience? Why did you feel that way? Which personal experiences did it remind you of?

Connecting to Information and Ideas

Continue to keep your brain active when you are working with information from both secondary and primary sources.

Examples of Secondary Sources		Examples of Primary Sources	
books	encyclopedias	interviews	maps
magazines	newspapers	diaries	photographs
Internet sites	videos	letters	blogs
textbooks		podcasts	surveys

Build understanding as you read, view, and listen by keeping notes. Use sticky notes or index cards to keep track of your thinking. You can sort them later and make more connections.

- Ask lots and lots of questions.
- Make inferences and predictions.
- Summarize big ideas.
- Add your own ideas.
- Make sketches.
- Record useful quotes.

- Fold a page in half. On one half jot down your questions and thoughts. On the other half make a visual of your notes (web, chart, graph, sketch, etc.).
- Fold a page in four. Respond to the prompts in each box.

I didn't know that…	Questions I have:
I disagree with…	I wonder…

Connecting to Media

The media have a big impact on everything you do. Learning how to analyze media and being aware of the uses and messages in media will help you become a better learner.

Make Comparisons

- compare an encyclopedia article and a nonfiction book
- compare several websites on a topic
- compare the book and movie version of a story
- compare newspaper articles from different papers
- compare speeches/podcasts from different experts
- compare photographs from different time periods
- compare different kinds of graphs
- compare interpretations by different artists

- ✔ What are you comparing? Why? Which parts are important to compare?
- ✔ Use a tool to help you sort your data (highlighters, sticky notes, index cards, graphic organizer). Find what is similar. Find what is different.
- ✔ Now organize your data.
- ✔ Study the similarities. Consider the differences. Can you draw any conclusions?
- ✔ What have you discovered? Why is it important?
- ✔ Share your discoveries.

Deconstruct Media

To make meaning, think about **text**, **audience**, and **production**.

What kind of media **text** is this?
- Who created this and why?
- What is the message or story?
- Who speaks and who is silent?
- Are there any stereotypes?
- What values are being promoted?

Media Meanings

What **production** techniques are used?
- What special effects are being used? For what purposes?
- What impact do these effects and techniques have?
- Who paid for and who profits from it?

Who is the target **audience** for this text?
- How can you tell?
- Whose point of view is represented? Do you feel the same way?
- Who is not represented?
- Do you feel manipulated? How?
- Would you buy this item/service? Why?

Learn more at Media Awareness Network
http://www.media-awareness.ca/english/index.cfm

Reading Smart

Make Use of Technologies

Learn how and when to use technologies to help you work better, faster, and more efficiently.

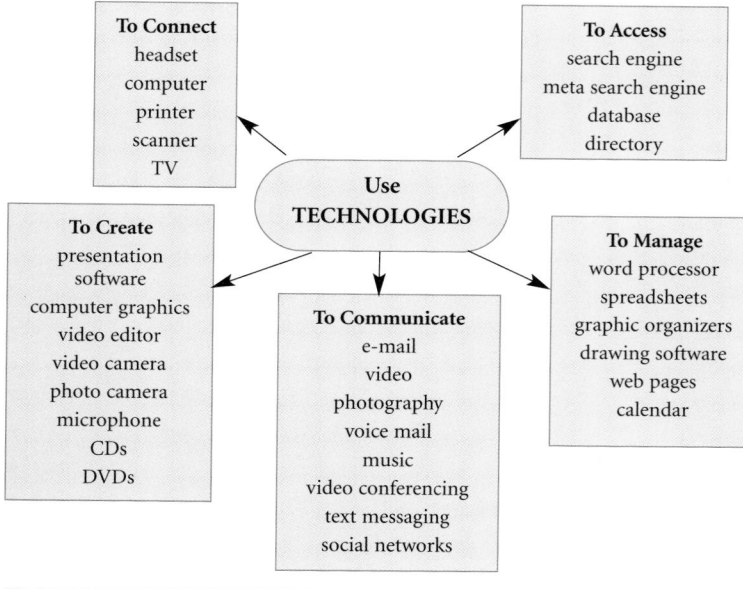

To Connect
headset
computer
printer
scanner
TV

To Access
search engine
meta search engine
database
directory

Use TECHNOLOGIES

To Create
presentation software
computer graphics
video editor
video camera
photo camera
microphone
CDs
DVDs

To Communicate
e-mail
video
photography
voice mail
music
video conferencing
text messaging
social networks

To Manage
word processor
spreadsheets
graphic organizers
drawing software
web pages
calendar

Look for websites and projects on the web to connect to people, places, and learning activities around the world (see Web Tools on page 29).

Be Webwise

Communicating, sharing ideas, searching for information, and playing on the Internet are important activities to build your learning skills. Just like in your home, at school, and out in your community, in this space you need to follow conduct codes. Be aware of potential dangers and develop some strategies for keeping safe on the net.

- Use a screen name; do not give your real name, address, school, phone number, or photo.
- Keep all your passwords private.
- Learn how to manage your virtual information spaces; e.g., block unwanted sites.
- Always be considerate and respectful of others.
- Talk to an adult you trust if you encounter anything that makes you feel uncomfortable or frightened.
- Assume all material on the Internet has copyright and reference any information you use.

Take Action
- Talk about how to stay safe on the Internet.
- Make your own list of safety tips.
- Create video of how to be cybersmart.
- Develop a comic strip about safe surfers.

Ten Steps in Searching Smart

To investigate your research questions, you will need to select the best sources of information and apply search strategies to find just the right information for your project. Here are ten steps in searching smart.

1. Review your question/focus statement.
2. Brainstorm for keywords. ***Create a web of keywords for searches on your topic.***
3. Look for synonyms or related terms; use a thesaurus.
4. Use proper names with caps; e.g., Leonardo Di Caprio.
5. Narrow or broaden search; e.g. dogs, canine.
6. Use Boolean searching; e.g. *and*, *or*, and *not*.
7. Test your search.
8. Scan results.
9. Revise search using different keywords if necessary.
10. Review exploration material for different keywords.

or		A *or* B	weather *or* storms
and		A *and* B	weather *and* storms
and not		A *and not* B	weather *and not* storms

Now think about the best search tools to address your information task:

- **Online Encyclopedias** are starting points for research.
- **Search engines** are effective when targeting information you know exists (e.g., places, organizations, people).
- **Directories** are useful when you are exploring a topic.
- **Periodical databases** are best when you are looking for current news and perspectives on issues and events.

Be Resource Wise

Before you decide to use a resource for your project, test its usefulness and reliability. Ask yourself:

- Who created it?
- When was it created or last updated?
- Does it look interesting?
- Is it easy to use?
- Can you trust this resource?

Examine for

- author, publisher, web moderator
- copyright date, references and/or Internet links
- reading ease, visuals
- table of contents, links, subtopics, glossary, index
- fact and/or opinion, evidence of bias or stereotyping

Will this resource be useful for your project? Why? Or why not?

People as Resources

Sometimes the best way to get the information you need is to ask an expert, conduct an interview, or develop a survey or poll.

1. Think about who you need to contact and why.
2. Listen to interviews on radio and TV, and read interviews in newspapers and magazines.
3. Examine examples of polls and surveys; the questions and the structure.
4. Experiment with the questions until you are sure they will glean the information you need.
5. Test your survey or interview questions with a friend.

Questioning Etiquette and Guidelines

Good questioners can get good results by simply using good manners. To become an effective questioner

- listen to the thoughts and ideas of others
- don't interrupt others
- be mindful of the feelings and the privacy of others
- be aware of your own feelings
- respect the rights and privacy of others
- show appreciation
- stay on topic

Using the Resources You Find

Work Honestly

Use this checklist to make sure that you are working honestly.

I am an honest learner because I
- ❏ understand that copyright is a law.
- ❏ know that I must credit all ideas, quotes, pictures, charts, maps, graphs, and music that I use.
- ❏ make sure that all other work is original.
- ❏ do not cut and paste information into my work.
- ❏ make my own notes and diagrams as I am researching.
- ❏ never copy anyone else's work.
- ❏ create my own research questions so my projects tell what I discovered.
- ❏ keep a source sheet of all the sources I use.
- ❏ put quotation marks around direct quotes.
- ❏ keep all my printouts from Internet sources.
- ❏ keep all interviews and surveys in my research folder.
- ❏ ask my teacher-librarian if I am not sure about copyright.

The best research uses a variety of reliable sources. Use the checklist on page 17 to keep track of where you got your information.

Resource Checklist

Things I have consulted:

- ❏ library holdings
- ❏ print encyclopedias
- ❏ online encyclopedias
- ❏ nonfiction books
- ❏ specialized reference books
- ❏ Internet sites
- ❏ online periodical database
- ❏ video
- ❏ TV programs
- ❏ magazines
- ❏ newspapers
- ❏ atlas
- ❏ almanac
- ❏ charts and posters
- ❏ pamphlets
- ❏ telephone book
- ❏ dictionary
- ❏ thesaurus
- ❏ _____
- ❏ _____
- ❏ _____

Places I have visited:

- ❏ school library
- ❏ public library
- ❏ reference library
- ❏ environmental organization
- ❏ museum
- ❏ art gallery
- ❏ government office
- ❏ historical site
- ❏ business
- ❏ _____

People I have talked to:

- ❏ teachers
- ❏ teacher-librarian
- ❏ reference librarian
- ❏ family
- ❏ friends
- ❏ community members
- ❏ experts on my topic
- ❏ politician
- ❏ environmental group

These resources worked best:

_____
_____
_____
_____
_____
_____
_____
_____
_____

Next time, I will…

_____
_____
_____
_____
_____
_____
_____
_____

READING TO RESEARCH

Building Understanding

Now that you have gathered lots of interesting information and ideas to answer your research question(s), it is time to take a closer look.

First determine if you have enough data. Are you pretty happy with what you have discovered so far? Have you examined your topic from different points of view? Have you kept accurate notes and referencing? Do you have any conflicting data? Is all your data on topic?

STOP and deal with any problems first.

You will be processing or thinking hard about your notes to build understanding.

Analyze

- sort and compare or classify
- look for patterns and trends
- find and examine relationships or connections
- determine cause and effect
- identify and predict impact
- interpret, infer, predict
- identify perspectives

Synthesize

- develop generalizations and report
- consider alternatives and make a judgment or prediction
- draw conclusions
- make decisions
- gain perspective and develop an argument or a thesis
- explore solutions and solve a problem or construct a new hypothesis

Processing Strategies

Make Connections
Reread your notes. Use highlighters, sticky notes, and index cards to help you keep track of your thinking (see page 12).

Organize your Thinking
Rework your highlighted notes and connections into an organizer to help you analyze it. As you organize and rearrange your data, you are helping your brain make new connections.

Conference
Set up a time with group members, your teacher, or your parents. Share your findings and test. Listen, respond, and question. Reflect on what was learned, what you still want to know, what was successful, and what you would like to improve.

See pages 19 to 21 for examples of visual organizers. Ask your teacher or teacher-librarian for blank organizers, find some on the Internet, or design your own.

Using Graphic Organizers

Organizing

Branch Diagram

- to break categories into smaller parts
- to graph family trees
- to plan organizational charts

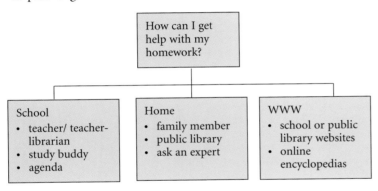

Comparing

Venn Diagram

- to examine details
- to make comparisons
- to organizer similarities and differences
- connect to what you read

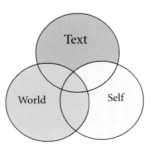

What's Different? What's the Same?

- to define criteria to make a vivid comparison

Comparing: Velcro and Burrs			
Comparison Criteria	**What's Different?**	**What's the Same?**	**What's Different?**
Origin	• man made		• natural occurrence
Purpose	• to hold things together	• to attach things	• to attach seeds to animals or people for distribution
Structure	• 2 pieces: 1 with hooks, 1 with loops • must be pressed together • pulls apart easily • doesn't break up	• small hooks • attaches well	• 1 piece with hooks • attaches without pressure • hard to pull off • breaks apart
Conclusion: The inventor of Velcro probably studied burrs to get ideas for his invention.			

Ordering

Series Line or Time Line

- to visualize a series of events
- to chart events in a story, novel, or film

Try creating two series or time lines to discover the relationships during a period of history.

Evolution of Cell Phones

Personal Handheld → E-mail Texting → Digital Photos → Video → Touch Screen

Making a Decision

T Chart

- to break down ideas
- to collect and organize data

Topic: Video Games	
That's Bad	**That's Good**
• take up lots of time • exercise only hands • produce Couch Potatoes • seem addictive • violent themes • stereotyping	• very entertaining • apply strategic thinking • can incorporate body movement • exercise joystick skills (used in robotics, surgery) • remote experiments (e.g., Mars)

Drawing Conclusions

Cross-Classification Chart

- to sort facts and find similarities
- to classify data and evaluate
- to make decisions or draw conclusions

Cross-Classification Chart								
What has been the impact of major tropical storms over the last century?								
Group Dates	Storm Name	Date	Category	Duration	Rainfall	Deaths	Evidence of Damage	$$$$ Damage
1900–1919								
1920–1939								
1940–1959								
1960–1989								
1990–								

Finding Solutions

ICE Diagram

- to explore a problem, and its causes and effects
- to propose a solution to an issue

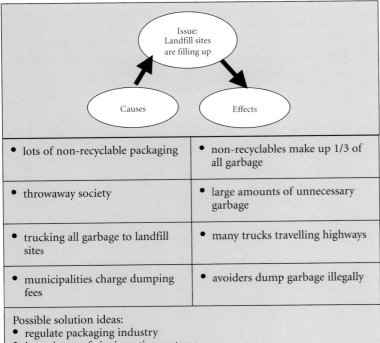

• lots of non-recyclable packaging	• non-recyclables make up 1/3 of all garbage
• throwaway society	• large amounts of unnecessary garbage
• trucking all garbage to landfill sites	• many trucks travelling highways
• municipalities charge dumping fees	• avoiders dump garbage illegally

Possible solution ideas:
- regulate packaging industry
- investigate safe incineration systems
- change throwaway habits

Flowchart

- to sequence historic events
- to plan a course of action
- to demonstrate a mathematical/ scientific process
- to write instructions

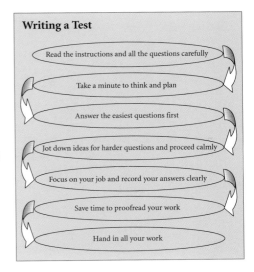

Reviewing for Study

Ranking Ladder

- to break ideas down into smaller and smaller pieces
- to demonstrate order or rank
- to find relationships
- to review information to study for tests

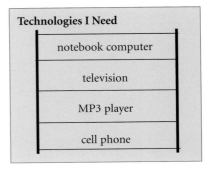

Creating Something New

Create something with your new knowledge and share it. Transform your understanding into a product or presentation so that others will have a chance to learn with you.

Review your research question(s) and consider what type of presentation would be the most powerful for getting your message across. Plan for the best result. Consider
- time needed to prepare and rehearse
- your audience
- your message
- assessment criteria
- materials and technologies needed
- location of presentation

Strategies for Sharing
Use these strategies to help you decide on a format.
- Consider your strengths: What do you do well?
- Create a visual: chart, brochure, model, poster, display
- Recreate a source: archive, timeline, costume, diary
- Write: poem, newspaper article, review, story, letter, report
- Present or perform: speech, newscast, debate, song, skit
- Take on a role: reporter, politician, activist, artist
- Design a game: puzzle, trivia, game board, quiz, crossword
- Use presentation technologies: slideshow, video, podcast
- Use collaborative technologies: blog, web page, video conference, e-mail

Presentation Checklist
- ❏ Decide on a format.
- ❏ Develop a plan.
- ❏ Write, sketch, or create a first draft/outline.
- ❏ Conference with a friend and make revisions if necessary.
- ❏ Prepare the final version of your presentation.
- ❏ Rehearse (with a friend, in front of a mirror, using a tape recorder, using a video camera).
- ❏ Time your presentation.
- ❏ Make revisions as necessary.
- ❏ Check and double check that you have everything you need.
- ❏ Be prepared to answer questions from your audience.
- ❏ Get a good rest the night before your presentation.
- ❏ **Be confident—you have something special to share!**

Measure your Research Success
Use these prompts to help you track your progress.
I wanted to…
I was successful in…
I had difficulty with…
Next time I will…
I am proud of…
I understand…
I want you to know that…
Because of my effort on this project, …
I am a better researcher now because…

Extension

You have seen and heard all the presentations. Now it's time for you and your class to reflect on everything you saw and heard. Do some more thinking about what you have learned from each other.

Think so what?

With a partner or in a small group discuss these questions.
- Are there relationships between our research discoveries?
- What are the similarities? What are the differences?
- What are the big ideas?
- Why is our research important? Who is it important to?
- What difference does it make to our community, to the world?
- What new questions do we have now?

Put all your new knowledge, ideas, and questions together so you can see the big picture about your topic. You might hold a debate, create a mural or collage, or build a class web.

Think what next?

- How can I/we use this information?
- What else do I/we want to know?
- How can I/we find out more?
- Who can help me/us?
- Where do I/we go from here?

Ask new questions. Do more research. Teach someone else. Share with an expert. Use or apply new learning. Take action. Keep on learning.

Working with Others

Learning how to work with a partner or a group is an important life skill. At school there are many opportunities to develop your collaborative skills:
- brainstorming; questioning
- research projects; experiments
- literature circles; information circles
- peer conferencing
- solving problems; making decisions; inventing something

Constructive IDEAS for Working in Groups

Invite lots of ideas to choose from.
- Aim for quantity.
- Select quality from quantity.

Defer judgment.
- Don't make positive or negative judgments.
- Don't use putdowns.

Expand
- Piggyback or hitchhike on the ideas of others.

Accept all ideas
- Record all suggestions.
- List ideas on paper, chalk board, computer, sticky notes, etc.

Stretch your thinking
- Be original.
- Try different approaches.
- Think from a different angle.

share your ideas and information

listen without interrupting

reflect on what you hear

show appreciation

encourage others

identify the strengths of others

enjoy the experience

respond to new ideas

make a plan and stick to it

accept responsibility for your task

remember: two heads are better than one

build on new ideas

be open to the ideas of others

practise considerate behavior

be aware of other people's feelings

seek others' opinions

Group Work is no puzzle. All the pieces fit!

When you work with a partner or in a group, you can achieve more in a shorter period of time.

Collaboration is a life skill.

Group Roles

Group members all have important roles and responsibilities.

When you are the Encourager

- ✔ Ask yourself: Is the group on track?
- ✔ Use positive body language: thumbs-up, nod, smile, etc.
- ✔ Use positive language: "Good job!" "That's it!" "Great idea." "Let's go for it." "Just a little more to do." "You are a great team!" "Keep thinking…"

When you are the Recorder

- ✔ Record all ideas.
- ✔ Don't comment or make judgments; just record.
- ✔ Use abbreviations and symbols to keep up.
- ✔ Ask for clarification if you are unsure of what was said.
- ✔ Paraphrase and confirm your interpretation.

When you are the Checker

- ✔ Make sure all group members understand their jobs.
- ✔ Ensure everyone understands the task.
- ✔ Check that you have all the materials/resources you need.
- ✔ Check the evaluation criteria.
- ✔ Ask: Have we completed everything?

When you are the Worrier

- ✔ Does the team agree on the task? Is the team staying on task?
- ✔ Is everyone contributing?
- ✔ When is the task due? How much time is left?
- ✔ Are we using our time wisely?
- ✔ Is everyone being considerate?
- ✔ Are we working as a team?
- ✔ Did we forget anything?

Using Learning Skills Everyday

Make learning part of your lifestyle. Apply learning skills to all facets of your life. Whenever you meet an information problem, remember the strategies for building Info Smarts. You need these skills every day when
• Purchasing a gift for a friend
• Deciding courses to pursue in high school
• Planning a party
• Considering sports/leisure activities to join
• Budgeting for a new bike, MP3 player, etc.
• Investigating volunteer positions
• Starting homework and assignments
And lots more…..

When you use your learning skills you will be able to
✔ Ask effective questions
✔ Think critically about information and ideas
✔ Process and manage information
✔ Use technologies effectively
✔ Work cooperatively and collaboratively
✔ Empathize with others
✔ Solve problems
✔ Make informed decisions
✔ Apply your knowledge to new situations
✔ Take initiative

Learning skills prepare you for success in the future. In all jobs you will need to use the skills you already have and continue learning.
• An auto mechanic has to be able to use diagnostic technologies and analyze them to fix a car.
• An intelligence agent must constantly update information and be able to ask strategic questions to prepare strategy.
• An animator is not only is creative, but also is able to apply knowledge to new situations in the virtual world.
• A meteorologist must process and manage a lot of information rapidly to make informed forecasts.
• A musician must work cooperatively and collaboratively with others to produce the desired effect.
• A human resources manager must be good at solving problems, and must also be able to empathize with others.

Brainstorm other careers. Try to match them with learning skills.

Into the Future

There may be new learning skills for you to explore, so be prepared.

Be ready to learn.

Using Learning Skills Everywhere

Organizing at Home
- Try out different spaces until you find the environment that works best for you (both physical and virtual space).
- Make your workspace your own with pictures and inspiring music.
- Create a bulletin board to post reminders and calendars.
- Keep work materials handy on a shelf, in a drawer, or in a basket.
- Use the public library.
- Ask family and friends when you need help.
- Prioritize and plan.
- Include time for fun.
- Get enough rest and exercise.
- Eat a well-balanced diet.

Keeping on Track at School
- Use a daily planner or agenda
- Record homework and due dates for each subject.
- Check your knapsack before leaving for home to make sure you have everything you need.
- Keep all your research material in a folder.
- Use your school library.
- Ask for help when you don't understand an assignment.
- Make wise use of your time.
- Prioritize what you must do, what you should do, and what you would like to do.

Letting Technologies Help
- Make up a weekly agenda template if you don't have one.
- Print calendars so you can plan ahead.
- Use your school and school library web page to help you locate resources.
- Learn how to keep track of favorite websites and online resources like encyclopedias and atlases.
- Save and organize your notes.
- Use graphic tools to make your learning visual.
- Learn to use spreadsheets to collect and organize information.
- Learn how to use multimedia tools and presentation software effectively.
- Connect to experts.

Keep on learning.

A Workout for Your Brain

You know that learning takes place in your brain. Your brain is something like a muscle, growing and getting stronger the more you use it. You are in charge of your brain, so it is up to you to put it to work using the exercises and strategies in *Building Info Smarts*:

- brainstorm information and ideas: page 4
- ask good thinking questions: pages 7, 8
- make connections to what you already know: page 12
- create a visual representation of your learning: page 19
- make predictions: pages 10, 12
- make comparisons: page 13
- create something new: page 22
- solve a problem: page 12, 18, 20, 26
- make a decision: page 18, 19
- think about what you are learning: page 18
- discover why your new knowledge is important: page 22
- set goals for improvement: page 22

Get Info Smart

- Discover and use your learning style.
- Keep *Building Info Smarts* handy during all research projects.
- Use study tips to energize your brain.
- Impress your teachers with your presentations.
- Boost your marks with graphic analyzers.
- Stay on track using contracts and planners.
- Build up your literacy skills.
- Target the experts with interviews and surveys.
- Explore technologies.
- Build teamwork skills.
- Think deeply with questions.
- Apply your effort potential.
- Remember that information can be found anywhere, all the time
- Think critically about things outside of school: media, movies, music, games, conversations.
- Apply your learning skills to your life.
- Reflect on your discoveries and successes.

Build a Web Bank

Create your own personal information bank of websites and virtual tools. Public libraries, government organizations, and museums all have great links for you. Refresh the sites often and delete the links that are no longer useful. Check out the following sites and add the ones you like to your personal web bank.

Safety on the Net

Be Web Aware http://www.bewebaware.ca/english/default.aspx
CyberSmart http://www.cybersmartkids.com.au/
Cyberethics for Kids http://www.cybercrime.gov/rules/kidinternet.htm

Homework Help

4twoExplore http://42explore.com/
Yahooligans http://www.yahooligans.com/
Ask for Kids http://www.askkids.com/
Info Please http://www.infoplease.com/
Canadian Encyclopedia http://www.thecanadianencyclopedia.com/
Internet Public Library http://www.ipl.org/
Homework Spot http://www.homeworkspot.com/

Research Projects

Research Helper http://www3.sympatico.ca/sandra.hughes/sandra.hughes/research/default.html
Infozone Research Skills http://www.pembinatrails.ca/infozone/
So You Have a Research Project
http://www.ri.net/schools/East_Greenwich/research.html#use%20the%20internet
Search Tools for Kids, Teens and Teachers http://eduscapes.com/tap/topic33.htm
NoodleTools
http://www.noodletools.com/debbie/literacies/information/5locate/adviceengine.html
Boolify http://www.boolify.org/index.php

Read, Write, and Think

The Learning Centre http://www.collectionscanada.gc.ca/education/008-2000-e.html
Kids Read http://www.kidsreads.com/reviews/index.asp
Electronic Books and OnLine Reading http://eduscapes.com/tap/topic93.htm
Merriam Webster Dictionary http://www.merriam-webster.com/
Graphic Organizers http://www.eduplace.com/graphicorganizer/index.html

Virtual Field Trips and Global Projects

World Wildlife Federation http://wwf.org/
National Geographic http://kids.nationalgeographic.com/
American Museum of Natural History http://www.amnh.org/
Nasa Quest Project http://quest.arc.nasa.gov/
Cyberschoolbus: a United Nations global learning project
http://www.un.org/Pubs/CyberSchoolBus/index.html

Index

Analyzing, 18
Brain
  Working out your, 28
Branch diagram, 19
Building info smarts, 28

Choosing resources, 11
Collaboration, 23, 24
Comparing, 13, 19
Conference, 18
Creating something new, 22–23
Cross-classification chart, 20

Drawing conclusions, 20

Essay, 5

Feelings
  Connecting to, 12
Fiction
  Actively reading/viewing/listening, 10
  Making connections to, 12
  Searching for, 11
  Finding solutions, 21
  Flowchart, 21

Graphic organizers
  Branch diagram, 19
  Cross-classification chart, 20
  Flowchart, 21
  ICE diagram, 21
  Ranking ladder, 21
  Series or time line, 20
  T chart, 20
  Types, 19–21
  Using, 19
  Venn diagram, 19
  What's different? What's the same?, 19
Group roles, 25

ICE diagram, 21
Internet
  Being smart about, 14
  Checklist, 10
  Directories, 15
  Online encyclopedias, 15
  Periodical databases, 15
  Safety, 14
  Search engines, 15
  Searching smart on, 15
  Tools for searching on, 15
  Web bank, 29

Learning
  Analyzing media, 13
  Exploring, 6–9
  From information to, 18–21
  Life, 26–27
  Methods of, 4
  Process equation, 5
  Responsible, 5
  Successful, 5
  Together, 22–25
  Understanding, 10
  Ways of, 4–5
Learning equation, 5
Learning log, 5
Learning profile, 4

Learning skills, 26–27
  Daily uses, 26
  Job-related, 26
  Keeping on track at school, 27
  Letting technologies help, 27
  Organizing at home, 27
  Results, , 26
  Using, 26–27
Library
  Choosing resources in, 11
  School, 9
Listening
  Active, 10, 12
  Connecting to, 12–13

Making comparisons, 13
Making connections
  Feelings, 12
  Fiction, 12
  Information and ideas, 12
  Media, 13
  Processing strategies, 18
  Making decisions, 20
Media
  Audience, 13
  Connecting to, 13
  Deconstructing, 13
  Meanings, 13
  Production, 13
  Types of, 10

Non-fiction
  Actively reading/viewing/listening, 10
  Searching for, 11
  Note-taking, 12, 18

Ordering, 20
Organizing, 19

Pre-research activities, 6
Presentations, 22–23
  Checklist, 22
  Extension, 23
  Thinking about, 23
  Processing strategies, 18
Profile
  Learning, 4
  Personal, 4
  Visual, 4
Project, 5

Question prompts, 7
Question stretchers, 8
Questioning etiquette, 16
Questions
  Asking, 23
  Deeper, 8
  Developing understanding, 8
  Digging, 8
  Etiquette and guidelines, 16
  Exploring, 7
  Relationship, 7
  Research (powerful), 8, 15, 18, 22
  Researching step-by-step, 8
  Simple, 8
  Starting, 7
  Surface, 8
  Topic-focused, 7
  Types, 7, 8

Ranking ladder, 21

Reading
  Active, 10, 12
  Connecting to, 12–13
  Research, 10–17
  Smart, 14–15
Report, 5
Research, 6
  Developing a plan for success, 6
  Focus or relationship words, 7
  Internet, 15
  Measuring success, 22
  Powerful questions, 7, 8, 18, 22, 23
  Reading to, 10–17
Resources
  Checklist, 17
  Choosing, 11
  People as, 16
  Usefulness and reliability of, 15
  Using, 15, 16
  Web, 29
Review, 5
  Study, 21

School library, 9
Series line, 20
Sharing strategies, 22
Sources
  Primary, 12
  Secondary, 12
  Statements of purpose, 7, 8
Story, 5
  Using a visual to map, 12
Summary, 5
Synthesizing, 18

T chart, 20
Teacher's expectations, 5
Technologies
  Collaborative, 22
  Developing learning skills with, 27
  Presentation, 22
  Using, 14
Thinking
  Organizing, 18
  Presentations, 23
  Stretching, 23
  Tracking, 12
  Time line, 20
Topics
  Exploring, 6
  Narrowing, 7
  Questions that focus on, 7

Understanding
  Building, 18
  Transforming, 22

Venn diagram, 19
Viewing
  Active, 10, 12
  Connecting to, 12–13

Web bank, 29
Web or mind map, 6
Working honestly, 16
Working smart, 5
Working with others, 23–25
  Constructive ideas for groups, 23
  Group roles, 25
  Puzzle, 24
Written products, 5

© 2008 Pembroke Publishers
538 Hood Road
Markham, Ontario, Canada L3R 3K9
www.pembrokepublishers.com

Distributed in the U.S. by Stenhouse Publishers
480 Congress Street
Portland, ME 04101-3400
www.stenhouse.com

We acknowledge the financial support of the Government of Canada through the Book
Publishing Industry Development Program (BPIDP) for our publishing activities.

We acknowledge the assistance of the OMDC Book Fund, an initiative of the Ontario
Media Development Corporation.

Library and Archives Canada Cataloguing in Publication

Koechlin, Carol
   Building info smarts : how to find and use all the stuff you need to make it through /
Carol Koechlin and Sandi Zwaan.

Includes index.
ISBN 978-1-55138-226-5

1. Information literacy — Study and teaching (Elementary).
2. Information literacy — Study and teaching (Secondary).
I. Zwaan, Sandi. II. Title.

ZA3075.K62 2008   028.7071   C2008-903732-4

Editor: Kat Mototsune
Cover design: John Zehethofer
Typesetting: Jay Tee Graphics Ltd.

Printed and bound in Canada
9 8 7 6 5 4 3 2 1

Thanks to
Rose Dodgson of Toronto District School Board
and
Diane Istead of Kawartha Pineridge District School Board
for their review and support

Some strategies have been adapted from earlier publications.
Loertscher, David; Koechlin, Carol; and Zwaan, Sandi (2007) *Beyond Bird Units*. Salt
Lake City, UT: Hi Willow Research and
   Publishing
— (2004) *Ban Those Bird Units*. Salt Lake City UT: Hi Willow
   Research and Publishing
Koechlin, Carol, and Zwaan, Sandi (2003) *Build Your Own Information Literate School*.
Salt Lake City UT: Hi Willow
   Research and Publishing, 2003.
— (1997) *Information Power Pack: Intermediate*. Markham, ON:
   Pembroke.
— (1997) *Information Power Pack: Junior*. Markham, ON:
   Pembroke.
— (1997) *Teaching Tools for the Information Age*. Markham, ON
   Pembroke.
— (2001) *Info Tasks for Successful Learning*. Markham, ON:
   Pembroke.
— (2006) *Q Tasks: How to Empower Students to Ask Questions
   and Care About Answers*. Markham, ON: Pembroke.

Carol Koechlin and **Sandi Zwaan** are award-winning authors,
experienced educators, and popular workshop presenters who have
dedicated their careers to helping students become better readers,
writers, and researchers. Their publications, including *Info Tasks
for Successful Learning* and *Q-Tasks: How to Empower Students
to Ask Questions and Care About Answers*, have been recognized
nationally and internationally as valuable tools for making
information and ideas more meaningful for students. Their
ongoing focus is developing instructional strategies and
information processes and facilities to address the evolving needs
of learners today.

This innovative flip book shows you how to build important information literacy skills as you learn to identify and take advantage of your unique learning style. You will learn how to apply what you read, hear, and see to what you already know, and grow in your understanding of your world.

In our amazing world, information is created and shared in many ways and *Building Info Smarts* offers strategies that will help you work in almost any format—from reading books and surfing the internet to working on a research project. The book suggests step-by-step approaches to finding the data you need and encourages you to build your own understanding so that your school work reflects original thought. It strives to help you go further and extend your learning, ask more questions, and become personally involved.

This handy book guides you beyond retelling information to help you become more confident in the information you experience and understand—making you info smart. The skills the book builds will support you throughout your school years and beyond.

An easy reference for students - an ideal review for teachers!

Pembroke Publishers Limited
538 Hood Road
Markham, ON L3R 3K9 Canada
www.pembrokepublishers.com

Front Cover Photo: Ajay Photographics

ISBN 978-1-55138-226-5

9 781551 382265

The Bully-Go-Round

Literacy and Arts Strategies for Promoting Bully Awareness in the Classroom

Larry Swartz

No single activity can change someone's behavior or attitude. When we implement literacy and arts approaches in the classroom, we invite students to connect, react, and respond to stories and information about issues and important events. As the complex issue of bullying continues to spin around the relationships of young people, we need to work toward a better understanding of it. We need to gain insight into why the bully behaves the way he or she does and to recognize that this person is capable of showing positive actions. We also need to investigate strategies to prepare ourselves for being caught in the triangle of the bully, the bullied, and the bystander.

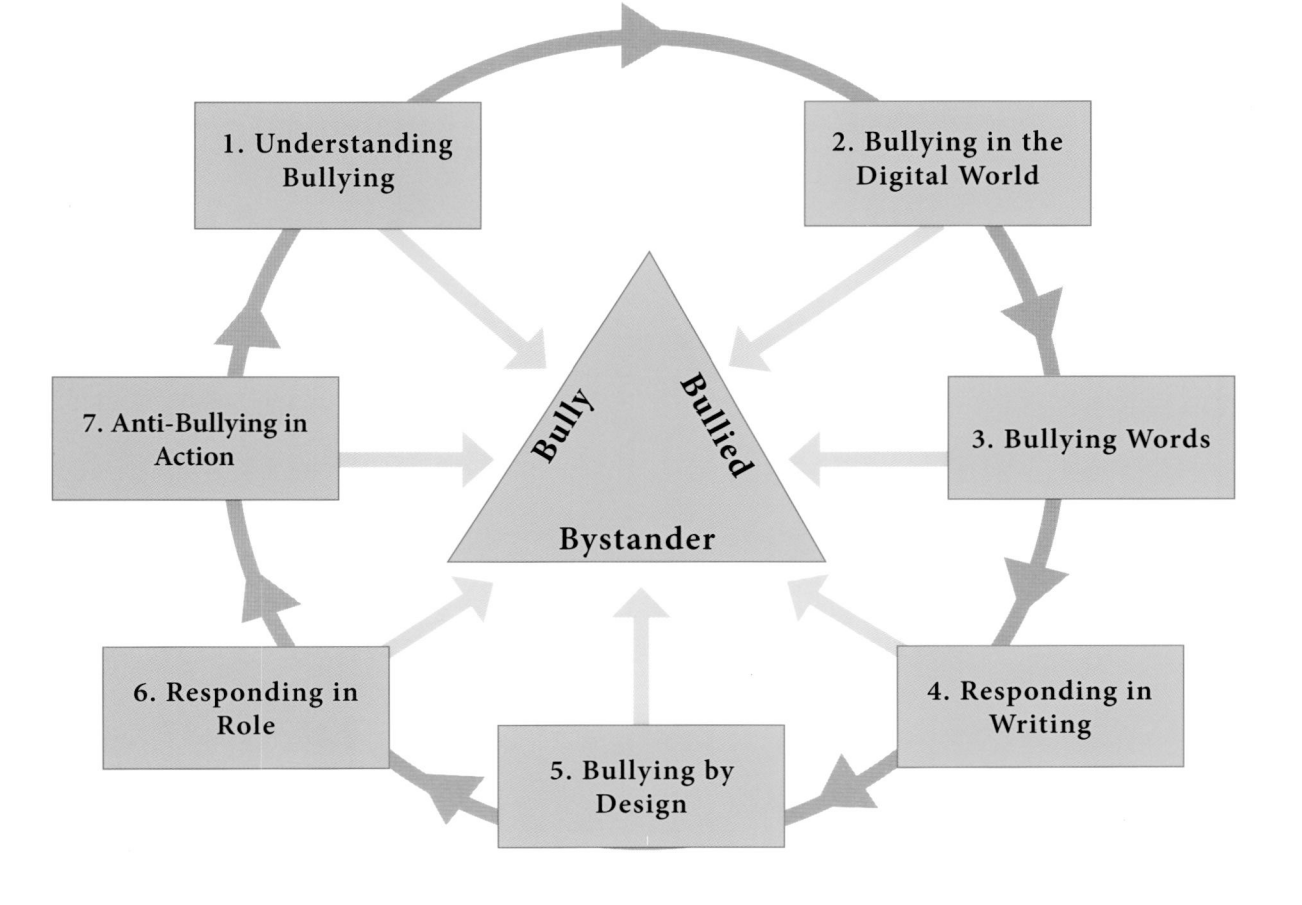